# Exciting British Recipes

Trustworthy Cookbook for Authentic
Traditional British Cooking

By

Angel Burns

# License Notices

# Table of Contents

# Traditional British Cooking
# Recipes

HHHHHHHHHHHHHHHHHHHHHHHHHHHHHHHHHHHHHHH

# Recipe 1: Super Eggs Benedict

This is a traditional English dish that I know you will want to serve nearly every breakfast. Packed full of authentic British flavors, I know you won't be able to get enough of it.

**Yield:** 4 servings

**Preparation Time:** 40 minutes

## Ingredient List:

- 4 spring onions
- Extra virgin olive oil, as needed
- 1 ½ cups of baby spinach, chopped
- 1 nutmeg, whole and grated
- 1 lemon
- 4 English muffins
- 8 eggs, beaten
- ½ cup of smoked ham, thinly sliced

## Ingredients for the hollandaise:

- ½ cup of butter
- 2 egg yolks
- 1 teaspoon of Dijon mustard
- White wine vinegar, as needed

HHHHHHHHHHHHHHHHHHHHHHHHHHHHHHHHHHHHH

**Instructions:**

1. Preheat the oven to 350 degrees.

2. In a frying pan set over low to medium heat, add in the spring onions. Drizzle 2 tablespoons of olive oil. Cook for 5 minutes or until soft.

3. Add in the spinach. Season with the nutmeg, dash of sea salt and black pepper. Stir well to mix. Add in a squeeze of lemon juice and cook for 1 to 2 minutes or until wilted.

4. In a saucepan set over medium heat, add in ½ cup of butter. Allow to melt.

5. In a bowl, add in the egg yolks. Set the bowl over a pot of hot water set over medium heat. Whisk the egg yolks roughly until foamy. Add in 1 tablespoon of the vinegar and season with a dash of salt and black pepper. Slowly add in the melted butter and continue to whisk vigorously.

6. Warm up the English muffins in the oven until warmed.

7. Poach the eggs in a medium saucepan filled with water set over medium heat. Simmer for 8 minutes or until the eggs are set.

8. Transfer the eggs onto the warm English muffins. Top off with the spinach and sliced ham. Drizzle the hollandaise sauce over the top. Serve immediately.

# Recipe 2: Filling Shepherd's Pie

This is a great tasting British dish you can make whenever you are craving something filling to make for a large group of people.

**Yield:** 8 servings

**Preparation Time:** 2 hours and 35 minutes

**Ingredient List:**

- Extra virgin olive oil, as needed
- 2 pounds of lamb shoulder, boneless and cut into small pieces
- Dash of salt
- ½ cup of all-purpose flour
- 2 leeks, cut into small pieces
- 3 ribs of celery, cut into small pieces
- 3 carrots, peeled and cut into small pieces
- 2 cloves of garlic, smashed
- ¼ cup of tomato paste
- 1 cup of red wine
- 3 to 4 cups of chicken stock
- 2 bay leaves
- 1 bundle of thyme
- 2 pounds of Yukon gold potatoes, cut into small pieces
- ¾ to 1 cup of heavy whipping cream
- 2 to 3 Tablespoons of cold butter, cut into small pieces
- 1 cup of peas, fresh or frozen

HHHHHHHHHHHHHHHHHHHHHHHHHHHHHHHHHHHHHHH

**Instructions:**

1. Place a large skillet over the medium to high heat. Grease with 1 tablespoon of olive oil.

2. Season the lamb shoulder with a dash of salt. Toss in the flour until coated on all sides. Place into the skillet. Cook for 5 minutes on each side or until browned. Remove and set aside. Drain the oil and wipe clean with a paper towel. Add in another tablespoon of olive oil.

3. Once hot, add in the chopped leeks, chopped celery and chopped carrots. Stir well to mix. Season with a dash of salt. Cook for 8 to 10 minutes or until soft. Add in the smashed garlic and continue to cook for an additional 2 minutes.

4. Add in the tomato paste and then cook for 3 minutes or until it begins to turn brown.

5. Add in the red wine. Cook for 2 minutes or until reduced by half. Add in the lamb and cover with chicken stock. Season with salt and add in the bay leaves and thyme. Cover and simmer for 1 hour or until the lamb is soft.

6. In a separate saucepan set over medium heat, add in the potatoes and cover with water. Season with a dash of salt and bring to a boil. Boil for 15 minutes or until the potatoes are soft. Drain and transfer into a food processor. Pulse on the highest setting until smooth in consistency.

7. In a separate small saucepan set over medium to high heat, add in the heavy whipping cream. Bring to a boil. Add in the cold butter and smooth potatoes. Season with a dash of salt and stir well until smooth in consistency. Remove from heat.

8. Add the frozen peas to the lamb. Continue to simmer or until the stock has been reduce. Discard the thyme and bay leaves.

9. Preheat the oven to broil.

10. Transfer the lamb into a large baking dish. Spread the mashed potatoes over the lamb mixture.

11. Place into the oven to broil for 3 to 5 minutes or until crispy.

12. Remove and allow to cool for 5 minutes before serving.

# Recipe 3: English Pork Pies

These hearty and delicious pie are typically served during lunch. What is best about them is that they are portable, making it perfect to take along with you whenever you are in a hurry.

**Yield:** 6 servings

**Preparation Time:** 2 hours and 15 minutes

**Ingredients for the filling:**

- 1 tablespoon of butter
- 2 teaspoons of salt
- 2 sprigs of thyme
- 1 onion, cut into small pieces
- ½ of a green apple, peeled and chopped into small pieces
- 2 cloves of garlic, minced
- 1 pound of pork butter, boneless and chopped into small pieces
- 4 ounces of bacon, thick cut and chopped
- 2 teaspoons of sage, chopped
- 1/2 teaspoons of black pepper
- ¼ teaspoons of ground mace
- ¼ teaspoons of grated nutmeg
- ¼ teaspoons of white pepper

**Ingredients for the dough:**

- 4 cups of all-purpose flour
- 6 Tablespoons of butter
- 6 Tablespoons of lard
- 1 ½ teaspoons of salt
- 1 egg yolk + 1 teaspoon of water, beaten together

**Instructions:**

1. In a skillet over low to medium heat, add in 1 tablespoon of butter. Once melted, add in ½ teaspoon of salt, sprigs of thyme, chopped onion and chopped green apple. Stir well to mix and cook for 5 minutes or until soft.

2. Add in the minced garlic and continue to cook for 2 minutes. Remove from heat and toss out the thyme. Set aside to cool completely.

3. In a large bowl, add in the apple mixture, pork butt, thick cut bacon, chopped sage, dash of black pepper, ground mace, grated nutmeg, remaining ½ teaspoons of salt and white pepper. Stir well to mix.

4. Transfer half of this mixture into a food processor. Pulse on the highest setting until a paste begins to form. Return back into the bowl with the remaining half of the mixture. Stir well until evenly mixed.

5. In a separate bowl, add in all of the ingredients for the dough along with 2/3 cup of water. Continue to stir until a dough begins to form.

6. Press ¼ cup of the dough into ramekins, shaping along the sides. Place the ramekins onto a large baking sheet.

7. Preheat the oven to 425 degrees.

8. Pour ½ cup of the meat filling into the ramekins. Brush the egg wash along the sides of the dough. Cover with 1/8 inch thick circles of the remaining dough and pinch the edges to seal. Brush the top of the pies with the egg wash.

9. Place into the oven to bake for 20 minutes. Reduce the temperature of the oven to 375 degrees. Continue to bake for 25 to 30 minutes or until golden.

10. Remove and set the pies aside to cool completely before serving.

# Recipe 4: Classic Fish and Chips

If there is one British dish that is as iconic as the country itself, it is fish and chips. This delicious dish can be made as a standalone meal or a tasty snack to enjoy any time of the day.

**Yield:** 4 servings

**Preparation Time:** 1 hour

**Ingredient List:**

- 1, 10 ounce box of green peas, frozen
- 2 Tablespoons of butter, cold
- 1 lemon, zest only
- Vegetable oil, for frying
- 2 pounds of russet potatoes, peeled and cut into batons
- 2 cups of all-purpose flour
- ½ cup of rice flour
- 1 teaspoon of baking soda
- ¾ cup of lager beer
- ¾ cup of sparkling water
- 1 teaspoon of lemon juice
- 1, 1 ½ pound fillet of hake, cut into small pieces
- Dash of salt and black pepper
- Malt vinegar, for serving

HHHHHHHHHHHHHHHHHHHHHHHHHHHHHHHHHHHHHH

**Instructions:**

1. In a medium saucepan set over medium heat, add in 6 cups of water. Season the water with salt and bring the water to a boil. Once boiling, add in the peas. Cook for 4 to 5 minutes. Drain the peas and reserve 3 tablespoons of the water. Place the peas back into the saucepan.

2. Add in the two tablespoons of cold butter, fresh lemon zest and reserved water. Season with a dash of salt and black pepper.

3. Mash carefully with a potato masher. Remove from heat and cover. Set aside.

4. In a large Dutch oven set over medium heat, pour in 2 inches of the vegetable oil. Heat the oil until it has reached 300 degrees.

5. Rinse the potatoes under running water to clean. Pat dry with a few paper towels. Add the potatoes into the pot and blanch for 2 minutes or until barely cooked through. Remove and transfer onto a large plate lined with paper towels to drain.

6. Increase the temperature of the oven to 345 degrees. Preheat the oven to 200 degrees.

7. In a large bowl, add in the all-purpose flour, rice flour, dash of salt and baking soda. Stir well to mix. Add in the lager, sparkling water and fresh lemon juice. Stir until just mixed.

8. Add the potatoes back into the hot oil. Fry for 4 minutes or until golden. Remove and drain on a large plate lined with paper towels. Season the potatoes with a dash of salt.

9. Season the hake fillets with a dash of salt and black pepper. Then dredge the fillets in the flour mixture. Dip into the batter until coated on all sides.

10. Add the fillets into the hot oil. Fry for 5 to 8 minutes or until golden and cooked through. Remove and transfer onto a large plate lined with paper towels to drain. Season the fillets with a dash of salt.

11. Serve the fish with the potatoes and mushy peas. Serve with the vinegar on the side.

# Recipe 5: Traditional Hot Cross Buns

This is a delicious and hearty bread dish that you can make in time for the Easter holiday season. It is so delicious, I know you will want to make them for nearly every holiday.

**Yield:** 12 servings

**Preparation Time:** 2 hours and 55 minutes

**Ingredient List:**

- ½ cup of water
- ½ cup of whole milk
- ½ cup of white sugar
- 4 ½ teaspoons of yeast
- 1/3 cup of butter, melted and extra as needed
- 1 egg yolk
- 1 ½ teaspoons of pure vanilla
- 3 cups of all-purpose flour
- ¾ teaspoons of fine salt
- ½ teaspoons of nutmeg, grated
- ½ teaspoons of powdered cinnamon
- ¼ teaspoons of ground ginger
- ½ cup of currants, plumped and cooled

**Ingredients for the glaze:**

- 2 cups of powdered sugar
- 2 Tablespoons of whole milk
- ¼ teaspoons of lemon zest, grated
- 1 teaspoon of pure vanilla

HHHHHHHHHHHHHHHHHHHHHHHHHHHHHHHHHHHHHH

**Instructions:**

1. In a saucepan set over low heat, add in the water and ½ cup of whole milk. Stir well to mx and cook until the milk reaches 100 degrees. Remove from heat.

2. Add in the yeast, dash of white sugar and dash of flour. Stir well to mix and set aside to rest for 30 minutes or until foamy.

3. In the yeast, add in the 1/3 cup of melted butter, egg yolk and pure vanilla. Whisk until evenly mixed.

4. In a separate bowl, add in the remaining 3 cups of flour, remaining ½ cup of white sugar, ¾ teaspoon of salt, ½ teaspoon of ground nutmeg, powdered cinnamon and ginger. Stir well to mix. Add in the yeast mixture and stir well until just mixed.

5. Grease a separate bowl with butter. Place the dough into the bowl and cover. Set aside to rise for 1 hour and 30 minutes.

6. Grease a baking dish with butter.

7. Remove the dough from the bowl and roll on a flat surface until it is 16 inches in length. Divide into 12 pieces and roll into a ball. Place into the baking dish. Cover and set aside to rise for 45 minutes.

8. Preheat the oven to 375 degrees.

9. Brush the tops of the buns with the beaten egg.

10. Place into the oven to bake for 25 minutes or until golden. Remove and set aside to cool for 5 minutes.

11. In a bowl, add in all of the ingredients for the glaze. Whisk until smooth in consistency.

12. Drizzle the glaze over the buns in a cross shape over each. Serve immediately.

# Recipe 6: Steak and Ale Pie

This is the perfect dish to make whenever you are craving something more on the filling side. It is perfect to make any day of the week.

**Yield:** 4 servings

**Preparation Time:** 1 hour and 5 minutes

**Ingredient List:**

- ½ of a 17.5 ounce pack of puff pastry
- 1 tablespoon of lard
- ½ pound of lean beef, cut into small cubes
- ¼ pound of carrots, chopped
- ¼ pound of turnips, chopped
- ½ pound of potatoes, peeled and chopped
- ¼ pound of onions, chopped
- 1 cup of water
- 1 cup of butter ale
- 1 tablespoon of cornstarch
- ¼ cup of cold water
- Dash of salt and black pepper

HHHHHHHHHHHHHHHHHHHHHHHHHHHHHHHHHHHHHH

**Instructions:**

1. Preheat the oven to 375 degrees.

2. In a large skillet set over medium to high heat, add in the lard. Once melted, add in the beef. Cook for 8 to 10 minutes or until browned on all sides. Remove the skillet from heat. Transfer the beef into a large baking dish.

3. Add the chopped carrots, chopped turnip, chopped potatoes and chopped onions in the baking dish. Stir well to mix.

4. In a small saucepan, add in 1 cup of water and 1 cup of the ale. Stir well to mix and bring the mixture to a simmer.

5. In a small bowl, add in ¼ cup of water and cornstarch. Whisk until smooth in consistency. Pour into the ale mixture and stir well to incorporate. Season with a dash of salt and cook for 3 minutes or until thick in consistency.

6. Pour the ale mixture over the beef.

7. Place the sheet of puff pastry over the top of the filling.

8. Place into the oven to bake for 45 to 50 minutes or until golden.

9. Remove and cool for 10 minutes before serving.

# Recipe 7: Royalty Chocolate Chips Scones

One bite of these scones and I know you will become hooked. The perfect way to satisfy your sweet tooth, this is a sweet dish that even British royalty would be envious of.

**Yield:** 12 servings

**Preparation Time:** 30 minutes

**Ingredient List:**

- 1 ¾ cup of all-purpose flour
- 1/3 cup of white sugar
- 2 teaspoons of baking powder
- ½ teaspoons of salt
- 5 Tablespoons of butter, chilled and cut into small cubes
- ½ cup of miniature semi-sweet chocolate chips
- 3 Tablespoons of orange juice

HHHHHHHHHHHHHHHHHHHHHHHHHHHHHHHHHHHHHHH

**Instructions:**

1. Preheat the oven to 400 degrees. Grease a large baking sheet with a cooking spray.

2. In a bowl, add in the all-purpose flour, dash of salt, white sugar and baking powder. Stir well to mix. Add in the butter and cut in with a pastry cutter until crumbly in consistency.

3. Add in the miniature chocolate chips and orange juice. Stir well until a dough begins to form.

4. Place the dough onto a flat surface that has been dusted with flour. Roll into a large 9 inch circle that is ½ an inch in thickness. Cut the dough into 2 ½ inch thick biscuits and place onto the baking sheet.

5. Place into the oven to bake for 12 to 15 minutes or until golden.

6. Remove and cool for 10 minutes before serving.

# Recipe 8: Yorkshire Gingerbread

This is the perfect dish for you to make for Christmas eve. It is so delicious, I know your friends and family will be begging you for the recipe.

**Yield:** 8 to 10 servings

**Preparation Time:** 49 hours and 30 minutes

**Ingredient List:**

- 8 ounces of self-rising flour
- 2 Tablespoons of ground ginger
- 1 tablespoon of ground allspice
- ½ teaspoons of salt
- 1 tablespoon of baking soda
- 4 ounces of butter, soft
- 4 ounces of light brown sugar
- 3 eggs, beaten
- 8 ounces of black treacle

HHHHHHHHHHHHHHHHHHHHHHHHHHHHHHHHHHHHH

**Instructions:**

1. Preheat the oven to 325 degrees. Grease a large baking dish with a cooking spray and line the bottom with a sheet of parchment paper.

2. In a large bowl, add in the self-rising flour, dash of salt, ground allspice and baking soda. Stir well to mix.

3. In a separate large bowl, add in the butter and light brown sugar. Beat with an electric mixer for 2 minutes or until creamy in consistency. Add in the beaten eggs and black treacle. Beat until mixed. Add in the flour mixture and continue to beat until evenly incorporated.

4. Pour the batter into the baking dish.

5. Place into the oven to bake for 50 minutes to 1 hour or until baked through.

6. Remove and set aside to cool for 10 minutes before serving.

# Recipe 9: British Pound Cake

This is a delicious pound cake dish you can make whenever you are craving something on the sweet side. Made with three different flavors, this is a dish that you will fall in love with.

**Yield:** 12 servings

**Preparation Time:** 1 hour and 30 minutes

**Ingredient List:**

- 3 cups of all-purpose flour
- ¼ teaspoons of baking soda
- ¼ teaspoons of salt
- 1 cup of butter, soft
- 3 cups of white sugar
- 6 eggs, beaten
- ½ teaspoons of pure vanilla
- ¼ teaspoons of orange extract
- ¼ teaspoons of almond extract
- 1 cup of sour cream

HHHHHHHHHHHHHHHHHHHHHHHHHHHHHHHHHHHHHH

**Instructions:**

1. Preheat your oven to 350 degrees. Grease a large tube pan with a cooking spray. Lightly dust with the flour.

2. In a large bowl, add in the all-purpose flour, baking soda and dash of salt. Stir well to mix and set this mixture aside.

3. In a separate large bowl, add in the butter and white sugar. Beat with an electric mixer until fluffy in consistency. Add in the eggs, pure vanilla, orange extract and almond extract. Continue to beat for 1 minute or until evenly incorporated.

4. Add in the baking soda mixture and sour cream. Continue to blend until evenly mixed.

5. Pour the batter into the tube pan.

6. Place into the oven to bake for 1 hour and 15 minutes until baked through.

7. Remove and cool for 10 minutes before serving.

# Recipe 10: Toffee Pudding

This is a classic dish that you can time for the Thanksgiving or Christmas season. It can be made in advance to save you some time.

**Yield:** 6 servings

**Preparation Time:** 1 hour and 20 minutes

## Ingredient List:

- All-purpose flour, for dusting
- 7 Tablespoons of butter, soft and extra for greasing
- 8 ounces of dates, chopped
- 1 cup + 2 Tablespoons of black tea
- 6 ounces of golden caster sugar
- 3 eggs, beaten
- 1 teaspoon of mixed spice
- 1 teaspoon of pure vanilla
- 8 ounces of self-rising flour
- ¾ teaspoons of baking soda
- Vanilla ice cream, for serving

## Ingredients for toffee sauce:

- 1 stick of butter, soft
- 9 ounces of light brown sugar
- 1 ¼ cups of golden syrup
- 1 cup of heavy whipping cream
- ½ teaspoons of pure vanilla

HHHHHHHHHHHHHHHHHHHHHHHHHHHHHHHHHHHHHHH

**Instructions:**

1. Preheat the oven to 350 degrees. Grease a large springform pan and dust lightly with flour. Line the bottom with a sheet of parchment paper.

2. In a large saucepan add in the chopped dates and black tea. Bring the mixture to a boil. Cook for 8 to 10 minutes or until soft.

3. In a large bowl add in the 7 tablespoons of butter. Beat with an electric mixer until fluffy in consistency. Add in the caster sugar, 3 eggs, mixed spice and pure vanilla. Continue to beat until fluffy.

4. Add in the date mixture, self rising flour and baking soda. Stir well until evenly incorporated.

5. Pour the mixture into the springform pan. Place into the oven to bake for 45 minutes or until baked through. Remove and set aside to rest for 5 minutes. Remove from the pan and transfer onto a large plate.

6. In a saucepan set over medium heat, add in the stick of butter. Once melted, add in the light brown sugar, golden syrup, heavy whipping cream and pure vanilla. Whisk until smooth in consistency. Boil for 5 minutes or until the sauce is thick in consistency. Remove from heat and set aside to cool for 5 to 10 minutes.

7. Serve the pudding with the toffee sauce drizzled over the top.

# Recipe 11: Chicken Takka Masala

This is a highly popular dish in Britain, to the point it is considered a national dish. It contains bold flavors that are incredibly hard to resist.

**Yield:** 4 servings

**Preparation Time:** 3 hours and 5 minutes

**Ingredient List:**

- 5 cloves of garlic, chopped
- 1, 1 ½ inch piece of ginger, peeled and chopped
- 2 teaspoons of coriander seeds
- 2 teaspoons of cumin seeds
- 1 cup of Greek yogurt
- 3 teaspoons of smoked paprika
- 2 teaspoons of lemon juice
- 1 ½ teaspoons of sugar
- ½ teaspoons of ground turmeric
- ¼ teaspoons of cayenne pepper
- Dash of salt and black pepper
- 1 ½ pounds of chicken thighs, boneless, skinless and chopped
- 3 Tablespoons of butter
- 1 onion, chopped
- 1 serrano pepper, thinly sliced
- 1, 28 ounce can of tomatoes, peeled and cut into quarters
- ¼ cup of heavy whipping cream
- 1 ½ teaspoons of garam masala
- 2 Tablespoons of cilantro, chopped
- White rice, steamed and for serving

**Instructions:**

1. Add the garlic and ginger into a food processor. Add in ¼ cup of water. Puree until a thick paste begins to form.

2. In a small skillet set over medium heat, add in the coriander and cumin seeds. Cook for 3 minutes or until fragrant. Transfer into the food processor. Pulse on the highest setting until finely ground.

3. In a large bowl, add in the 2 tablespoons of the garlic paste, 2 teaspoons of the ground cumin and coriander mixture, Greek yogurt, 1 ½ teaspoons of the smoked paprika, fresh lemon juice, ½ teaspoon of white sugar, ¼ teaspoon of ground turmeric, cayenne pepper and dash of salt and black pepper. Stir well to mix and add in the chicken thighs. Toss well to coat.

4. Cover and place into the fridge to marinate for 2 to 4 hours.

5. In a large Dutch oven set over medium heat, add in the three tablespoons of butter. Once melted, add in the chopped onions and sliced serrano pepper. Cook for 5 minutes or until soft.

6. Add in 2 tablespoons of the ginger paste and remaining cumin mixture. Add in the remaining smoked paprika and turmeric. Stir well to mix and cook for 3 minutes.

7. Add in the remaining white sugar, chopped tomatoes and 1 ½ cups of water. Stir well to mix and simmer for 25 minutes.

8. Preheat the oven to broil.

9. Remove the chicken from the fridge and place onto a large baking sheet. Season with a dash of salt and black pepper. Place into the oven to broil for 5 minutes. Flip the chicken and continue broiling for 5 minutes or until the chicken has been cooked through. Remove and transfer the chicken into a large bowl.

10. In the sauce in the Dutch oven, add in the garam masala and heavy whipping cream. Stir well to incorporate. Cook for 5 minutes. Remove from heat and pour over the broiled chicken.

11. Add in the chopped cilantro and toss to coat.

12. Serve the chicken with the steamed rice.

# Recipe 12: Tarragon Chicken Salad Sandwiches

If you want to host a Sunday brunch, then these are the perfect sandwiches for you to make for your guests. Feel free to top these sandwiches off with your favorite toppings.

**Yield:** 6 servings

**Preparation Time:** 1 hour and 15 minutes

**Ingredient List:**

- 4 cups of chicken, cooked and shredded
- ½ cup of mayonnaise
- ¼ cup of sour cream
- 1 tablespoon of tarragon, chopped
- ½ cup of red grapes, chopped
- ¼ cup of pecans, chopped
- Dash of salt and black pepper
- 12 whole wheat bread slices, crusts removed

HHHHHHHHHHHHHHHHHHHHHHHHHHHHHHHHHHHHHHH

**Instructions:**

1. In a medium bowl, add in the shredded chicken, mayonnaise, chopped tarragon and sour cream. Season with a dash of salt and black pepper. Stir well until evenly mixed.

2. Add in the chopped pecans and chopped red grapes. Stir well until evenly incorporated.

3. Cover and set into the fridge to chill for 1 hour.

4. Scoop the chicken mixture onto each slice of whole wheat bread. Bring two of the slices of bread together to form sandwiches.

5. Slice into triangles and serve immediately.

# Recipe 13: Cream Tea Cakes

This is another dish you can serve during tea time that I know you will want to make as often as possible. Be sure to serve these cakes with raspberry jam for the tastiest results.

**Yield:** 9 servings

**Preparation Time:** 40 minutes

**Ingredient List:**

- 1 cup of margarine
- ¾ cup of white sugar
- 2 ¼ cups of self-rising flour
- 4 Tablespoons of powdered custard
- 1 egg, beaten
- Dash of salt

HHHHHHHHHHHHHHHHHHHHHHHHHHHHHHHHHHHHHHH

**Instructions:**

1. Preheat the oven to 350 degrees.

2. In a medium bowl, add in the margarine and white sugar. Beat with an electric mixer until fluffy in consistency.

3. Add in the beaten egg, powdered custard, self-rising flour and dash of salt. Continue to beat until a dough begins to form.

4. Transfer the dough on a flat surface dusted with the flour. Knead for 1 to 2 minutes or until the dough is smooth.

5. Roll out the dough into a large rectangle that is ½ an inch in thickness. Cut out 9 biscuits using a biscuit cutter. Place the biscuits onto a large baking sheet.

6. Place into the oven to bake for 10 minutes or until browned.

7. Remove and cool for 5 minutes before serving.

# Recipe 14: Beef and Ginger Meat Pasties

This is a filling and delicious dish you can make whenever you are craving something exotic. Inspired by classic Mexican empanadas, this is a dish that is hard to resist.

**Yield:** 12 servings

**Preparation Time:** 1 hour

**Ingredient List:**

- 1 crust pastry
- 2 Tablespoons of extra virgin olive oil
- 5 ounces of onions, peeled and chopped
- 2 cloves of garlic, peeled and chopped
- 1 teaspoon of ginger root, grated
- Dash of salt and black pepper
- 1 teaspoon of coriander seeds
- 1 teaspoon of cumin seeds
- 1 teaspoon of black mustard seeds, optional
- 7 ounces of lean ground beef
- 1 tablespoon of tomato puree
- 1 tablespoon of English mustard
- 1 teaspoon of Worcestershire sauce
- 3 ½ ounces of peas, fresh or frozen
- 1 tablespoon of mint leaves, chopped
- 1 egg, beaten

HHHHHHHHHHHHHHHHHHHHHHHHHHHHHHHHHHHHHHHH

**Instructions:**

1. Preheat the oven to 425 degrees.

2. In a large saucepan set over medium heat, add in the olive oil. Once hot, add in the chopped onion, chopped garlic, chopped ginger, dash of salt and dash of black pepper. Stir well to mix. Cook for 5 minutes or until soft.

3. In a mortar, add in the coriander seeds and cumin seeds. Grind with a pestle until finely ground. Transfer into the saucepan.

4. Add in the ground beef, tomato puree, English mustard and Worcestershire sauce. Stir well to mix and cook for 15 minutes or until the beef is browned. Add in the frozen peas and cook for 1 to 2 minutes.

5. Add in the mint and season with a dash of salt and black pepper. Stir well to evenly mix. Remove and set aside to cool.

6. Roll out the crust pastry on a flat surface dusted with flour until 1/16 inch in thickness. Use a biscuit cutter and cut out circles that are 4 ½ inch in thickness.

7. Add a tablespoon of the beef mixture into the center of each pastry. Spread the edges with the beaten egg and fold over the filling. Crimp the edges. Repeat with the remaining dough and filling. Transfer onto a large baking sheet.

8. Spread the remaining beaten egg over the top of each pasty.

9.Place into the oven to bake for 15 to 20 minutes or until golden.

10. Remove and cool for 10 minutes before serving.

# Recipe 15: English Carrot Pudding

This is a classic English dish that has been around for as long as the dynasty itself. It is incredibly moist and packed full of a flavor I know you will love.

**Yield:** 12 servings

**Preparation Time:** 4 hours and 20 minutes

**Ingredient List:**

- ½ cup of shortening
- 1 cup of white sugar
- 1 ½ cups of white flour
- 1 teaspoon of baker's style baking soda
- ¾ teaspoons of salt
- 1 teaspoon of powdered cinnamon
- 1 teaspoon of ground nutmeg
- ½ teaspoons of powdered cloves
- 1 cup of carrots, grated
- 1 cup of golden raisins
- 1 cup of walnuts, chopped
- ¾ cup of white sugar
- 1 ½ teaspoons of cornstarch
- Dash of salt
- 1 ¼ cups of hot water
- 3 ½ teaspoons of butter, soft
- 3 ½ teaspoons of fresh lemon juice
- 1 ½ teaspoons pure vanilla

HHHHHHHHHHHHHHHHHHHHHHHHHHHHHHHHHHHH

**Instructions:**

1. In a large bowl, add in the shortening and 1 cup of white sugar. Beat until fluffy in consistency.

2. Add in the all-purpose flour, baking soda, ground cloves, dash of salt, ground cinnamon and ground nutmeg. Stir well until evenly incorporated.

3. Add in the carrots, golden raisins and walnuts. Fold until evenly mixed.

4. Pour the batter into a large pudding mold. Cover with a sheet of aluminum foil. Transfer the pan into a large Dutch oven filled with 2 inches of water and set over low heat.

5. Simmer for 4 ½ hours. Remove from heat and set aside.

6. In a small saucepan, ass in the cornstarch, dash of salt and ¾ cup of white sugar. Stir well until mixed. Add in the hot water, fresh lemon juice and pure vanilla. Stir well to incorporate. Cook for 5 minutes or until thick in consistency.

7. Pour the sauce over the pudding and serve immediately.

# Recipe 16: Plum Pudding

This is the perfect sweet dish to make whenever you need something delicious for a special occasion. One bite and your friends and family will be begging you for the recipe.

**Yield:** 10 to 12 servings

**Preparation Time:** 4 hours and 30 minutes

**Ingredients for the pudding:**

- 1 cup of white flour
- Dash of salt
- ½ teaspoons of powdered nutmeg
- ½ teaspoons of powdered cinnamon
- ½ teaspoons of cloves
- ½ teaspoons of powdered allspice
- ½ teaspoons of baker's style baking soda
- 1 cup of bread crumbs
- 1 cup of suet, chopped
- 1 cup of prunes, pulp only
- ½ cup of light brown sugar
- 1 cup of prunes, chopped
- ¼ cup of lemon peel, chopped
- ¼ cup of molasses
- 3 eggs, separated

**Ingredients for the sauce:**

- ¼ cup of butter, soft
- 1 cup of powdered sugar
- 1 tablespoon of dark rum
- ½ teaspoons pure vanilla

## Instructions:

1. In a large bowl, add in all of the ingredients for the pudding. Beat with an electric mixer on the medium setting until smooth in consistency.

2. Grease a large pudding mold with a cooking spray and pour the batter into it. Cover with a sheet of aluminum foil.

3. In a large Dutch oven, fill with 2 inches of water. Set over low heat and add the pudding mold into it. Cover and steam for 3 to 4 hours or until cooked through.

4. In a medium bowl, add in the ¼ cup of soft butter, 1 cup of powdered sugar, tablespoon of rum and ½ teaspoon pure vanilla. Beat with an electric mixer until pale.

5. Pour the sauce over the cooked pudding. Serve immediately.

# Recipe 17: Herbed Yorkshire Pudding

This is a classic and delicious British dish you will want to serve any night of the week. It is so delicious, even the pickiest people in your home won't be able to get enough of it.

**Yield:** 6 to 8 servings

**Preparation Time:** 40 minutes

**Ingredient List:**

- 3 eggs, beaten
- 1 ¼ cups of whole milk
- 1 ¼ cups all-purpose flour
- 3 Tablespoons of chives and parsley, mixed together
- Dash of salt and black pepper
- ¼ cup of beef drippings

HHHHHHHHHHHHHHHHHHHHHHHHHHHHHHHHHHHHHH

**Instructions:**

1. Preheat the oven to 350 degrees.

2. Grease a baking dish into the oven. Heat up for 10 minutes.

3. In a large bowl, add in the beaten eggs. Continue to whisk until foamy.

4. Add in the whole milk, flour, mixed herbs, dash of salt and dash of black pepper. Whisk until smooth in consistency.

5. Pour the beef drippings into the baking dish. Pour the batter over the top.

6. Place into the oven to bake for 10 minutes. Reduce the temperature of the oven to 350 degrees. Continue to bake for 15 to 20 minutes or until browned.

7. Remove and serve immediately.

# Recipe 18: English Muffin Bread

If you are looking to make an easy and delicious bread recipe, then this is the perfect dish for you to make. It is perfect to serve early in the morning.

**Yield:** 20 servings

**Preparation Time:** 1 hour and 25 minutes

**Ingredient List:**

- 2 cups of whole milk
- ½ cup of water
- 2 Tablespoons of cornmeal
- 6 cups of bread flour
- 2, .25 ounce pack of yeast
- 1 tablespoon of white sugar
- 2 teaspoons of salt
- ¼ teaspoons of baking soda

HHHHHHHHHHHHHHHHHHHHHHHHHHHHHHHHHHHHH

**Instructions:**

1. Grease two large loaf pans with a cooking spray. Sprinkle the cornmeal into the pans.

2. In a large bowl, add in 3 cups of the bread flour, dash of salt, pack of yeast and baking soda. Stir well to mix.

3. Add in the whole milk and remaining flour. Continue to mix until evenly blended and a dough begins to form.

4. Pour the batter into the loaf pans. Cover and set aside to rise for 45 minutes.

5. Preheat the oven to 400 degrees.

6. Place the loaf pans into the oven to bake for 25 minutes or until golden. Remove and set aside to cool for 10 minutes before serving.

# Recipe 19: Classic Bangers and Mash

This is a delicious British dish that you can often find served in many British pubs. It is great for those potato lovers in your home.

**Yield:** 4 servings

**Preparation Time:** 2 hours

**Ingredients for the bangers:**

- 3 feet long hog casings, optional
- ½ teaspoons of white pepper
- 1 ½ pounds of pork butter, boneless and cut into small cubes
- 8 ounces of fat back, cut into small cubes
- ¼ cup of onion, grated
- 3 ½ teaspoons of salt
- 2 teaspoons of sage, chopped
- 1 teaspoon of black pepper
- 1/8 teaspoons of ground ginger
- 1/8 teaspoons of ground nutmeg
- ¼ cup of breadcrumbs
- ¼ cup of chicken stock, cold
- 1 teaspoon of honey
- 1 tablespoon of vegetable oil
- 1 ½ pounds of Yukon gold potatoes, peeled and cut into small pieces
- Dash of salt
- ½ cup of whole milk, hot
- 1/3 cup of heavy whipping cream, hot

**Ingredients for the mash:**

- 5 Tablespoons of cold butter, cut into small pieces
- 1 ½ Tablespoons of chives, chopped

**Ingredients for the gravy:**

- 2 Tablespoons of butter
- 2 cups of onion, chopped
- 2 Tablespoons of all-purpose flour
- 1 clove of garlic, minced
- 2 cups of chicken stock
- 1 teaspoon of Worcestershire sauce
- Dash of salt and black pepper

HHHHHHHHHHHHHHHHHHHHHHHHHHHHHHHHHHHHHH

**Instructions:**

1. Rinse the hog casings under water. Then transfer into a large bowl and cover with cold water. Set aside to soak for 2 hours.

2. In a medium bowl, add in the pork butter, fatback, grated onions, dash of salt, chopped sage, black pepper, ½ teaspoon of white pepper, ground ginger and ground nutmeg. Stir well to mix. Transfer this mixture into the freezer and chill for 30 minutes or until crunchy.

3. Place the potatoes into a Dutch oven. Cover with water. Simmer over medium to high heat. Season with a dash of salt. Simmer for 10 to 12 minutes or until the potatoes are cooked through.

4. Drain the potatoes and transfer into a large bowl. Mash thoroughly until smooth in consistency. Add in the ½ cup of milk, heavy whipping cream and 5 tablespoons of butter. Season with the chives and dash of salt. Continue to mash until smooth in consistency.

5. Use a meat grinder set with a medium die and grind the pork into a medium bowl.

6. In a small bowl, add in the breadcrumbs, ¼ cup of chicken stock and honey. Whisk to mix and add into the pork mixture. Stir well until incorporated.

7. Stuff the casings with the pork mixture and twist the ends of the casings to seal.

8. Preheat the oven to 170 degrees.

9. In a large saucepan set over medium heat, add in 4 inches of water. Bring to a simmer. Add in the links and poach for 5 minutes. Remove and pat dry with a few paper towels.

10. In a separate skillet set over medium heat, add in the tablespoon of vegetable oil. Once hot, add in the links and cook for 5 minutes or until crispy. Transfer immediately onto a large baking sheet and place into the oven to keep warm.

11. In a medium skillet set over medium heat, add in 2 tablespoons of butter. Once melted, add in 2 cups of onion. Cook for 15 minutes or until golden. Add in 2 tablespoons of all-purpose flour and 1 clove of minced garlic. Stir well to mix and cook for 2 minutes.

12. Add in 2 cups of chicken stock and 1 teaspoon of Worcestershire sauce. Stir well to mix. Cook for 10 minutes. Season with a dash of salt and black pepper.

13. Serve the bangers immediately with the mashed potatoes and gravy drizzled over the top.

# Recipe 20: Sweet Pecan Pasties

This is a tasty and sweet dish you can make just in time for the holiday season. It is so delicious, I guarantee these treats would be gone in just a matter of a few minutes.

**Yield:** 24 servings

**Preparation Time:** 1 hour and 55 minutes

**Ingredient List:**

- ½ cup of butter, soft
- 1 tablespoon of butter, melted
- 1, 3 ounce pack of cream cheese, soft
- 1 cup all-purpose flour
- 1 egg, beaten
- ¾ cup of light brown sugar
- 1 teaspoon of pure vanilla
- Dash of salt
- ½ cup of pecans, chopped

HHHHHHHHHHHHHHHHHHHHHHHHHHHHHHHHHHHHHHH

**Instructions:**

1. In a medium bowl, add in ½ cup of soft butter and the cream cheese. Beat with an electric mixer for 2 minutes or until smooth in consistency. Add in the all-purpose flour and continue to beat until evenly mixed. Cover and set into the fridge to chill for 1 hour.

2. Preheat the oven to 325 degrees. Grease a miniature muffin pan with a cooking spray.

3. In a large bowl, add in the 1 tablespoon of melted butter, beaten egg, light brown sugar, pure vanilla and dash of salt. Stir well until smooth in consistency. Set this mixture aside.

4. Remove the dough from the fridge and shape into balls that are 1 inch in diameter. Press the balls into the bottom of each muffin cup, spreading evenly all the sides.

5. Spoon 1 teaspoon of pecans into each muffin cup and fill with the brown sugar mixture.

6. Place into the oven to bake for 25 minutes or until set.

7. Remove and cool for 10 minutes before serving.

# Recipe 21: Classic British Crumpets

This is a delicious and classic British dish you can serve with your next cup of coffee or tea. One bite and you will feel as if you are sitting right in the middle of London.

**Yield:** 4 to 6 servings

**Preparation Time:** 2 hours and 45 minutes

## Ingredient List:

- 3 ½ cups all-purpose flour
- 1 ¼ cups of water, warm
- 1 ¼ cups of whole milk
- 2 Tablespoons of butter, melted and cooled
- ½ teaspoons of baking powder
- 1 tablespoon of clover honey
- 2 ½ teaspoons of yeast
- ½ teaspoons of sea salt

## Ingredients for the whipped butter:

- 1 cup of heavy whipping cream
- Dash of sea salt

НННННННННННННННННННННННННННННННННННННННННН

**Instructions:**

1. In a large bowl of a stand mixer, add in the whole milk, all-purpose flour, cooled butter, clover honey, yeast, dash of salt and baking powder. Beat with an electric mixer until smooth in consistency. Continue to beat using a dough hook until a dough forms.

2. Transfer the dough to a greased bowl. Cover and set aside to rise for 1 hour.

3. Grease a large skillet with a cooking spray and set over medium heat. Grease metal biscuit rings with a cooking spray and place directly into the skillet. Pour the batter into the rings. Cook for 5 minutes or until golden.

4. Remove the rings from the crumpets and flip the crumpets. Continue to cook for an additional 5 minutes. Remove the crumpets and set aside.

5. In a small bowl of a stand mixer, add in the heavy whipping cream and dash of sea salt. Beat on the highest setting until fluffy in consistency. Remove and transfer into the fridge to chill for 15 minutes before using.

6. Slather the crumpets with the whipped butter and serve immediately.

# Recipe 22: Victoria Sponge Cake

This is a delicious cake dish that even Queen Victoria would have been envious of. Incredibly moist and light, this is a dish everybody will loves once they try it.

**Yield:** 8 servings

**Preparation Time:** 1 hour and 25 minutes

**Ingredient List:**

- 1 tablespoon of butter, soft and evenly divided

**Ingredients for the cake:**

- ¾ cup of butter, soft and extra for greasing
- ¾ cup of white sugar
- 3 eggs, beaten
- 1 teaspoon of pure vanilla
- 1 ¼ cups all-purpose flour
- 1 teaspoon of baking powder
- ½ teaspoons of salt

**Ingredients for filling:**

- 1/3 cup of powdered
- ¼ cup of butter, soft
- 1 teaspoon of pure vanilla
- 1/3 cup of raspberry jam, seedless

HHHHHHHHHHHHHHHHHHHHHHHHHHHHHHHHHHHHHH

**Instructions:**

1. Preheat the oven to 350 degrees. Grease two large cake pans with butter. Line the bottom of the cake pans with sheet of parchment paper.

2. In a large bowl of a stand mixer, add in ¾ cup of butter and white sugar. Beat on the medium setting until fluffy in consistency. Add in the eggs and pure vanilla. Beat for 2 minutes or until smooth in consistency.

3. Add in the all-purpose flour, dash of salt and baking powder. Fold gently until incorporated.

4. Pour the batter between the two cake pans.

5. Place into the oven to bake for 20 minutes or until golden. Remove and cool in the pans for 5 minutes before inverting onto a wire rack to cool for 30 minutes.

6. In a medium bowl, add in the powdered sugar, ¼ cup of remaining butter and teaspoon of pure vanilla. Beat with an electric mixer until smooth in consistency.

7. Spread the filling over one of the cakes. Spread the raspberry jam over the filling. Place the second cake over the top and serve immediately.

# Recipe 23: Classic Treacle Tart

This is a delicious dish that every Harry Potter fanatic will be familiar with. One bite of this dish and you will never want to put it down.

**Yield:** 8 servings

**Preparation Time:** 45 minutes

**Ingredient List:**

- 1, 9 inch pie crust
- 1 cup of golden syrup
- ¼ cup of heavy whipping cream
- 1 cup of bread crumbs
- 1 lemon, fresh and zest only
- 2 Tablespoons of fresh lemon juice

HHHHHHHHHHHHHHHHHHHHHHHHHHHHHHHHHHHHHHH

**Instructions:**

1. Preheat the oven to 375 degrees.

2. Place the pie crust into a large pie plate.

3. In a large bowl, add in the golden syrup, heavy whipping cream, bread crumbs, fresh lemon zest and fresh lemon juice. Stir well until evenly mixed. Pour the batter into the pie crust.

4. Place into the oven to bake for 35 to 40 minutes.

5. Remove and cool for 10 minutes before serving.

# Recipe 24: Simple British Scones

This is another delicious scone dish you can serve to enjoy with your morning or afternoon tea. It is incredibly easy to make, even those new to cooking will be able to make it with ease.

**Yield:** 12 servings

**Preparation Time:** 25 minutes

**Ingredient List:**

- 2 cups of white flour
- 1 teaspoon of cream of tartar
- ½ teaspoons of baker's style baking soda
- Dash of salt
- ¼ cup of margarine
- 1/8 cup of white sugar
- ½ cup of whole milk
- 2 Tablespoons of whole milk

HHHHHHHHHHHHHHHHHHHHHHHHHHHHHHHHHHHHHHHH

**Instructions:**

1. Preheat the oven to 425 degrees. Line a large baking sheet with a sheet of parchment paper.

2. In a bowl, add in the all-purpose flour, cream of tartar, dash of salt and baking soda. Stir well to mix. Add in the butter and sugar. Cut in with a pastry cutter until crumbly in consistency.

3. Add in the ½ cup of whole milk and stir well until a dough begins to form.

4. Place the dough onto a flat surface that has been dusted with flour. Roll until ¾ inch in thickness. Cut 2 inch rounds out of the dough and place onto the baking sheet. Brush the top of the biscuits with the 2 tablespoons of milk.

5. Place into the oven to bake for 10 minutes.

6. Remove and transfer to a wire rack to cool for 5 to 10 minutes before serving.

# Recipe 25: Welsh Cookies

One bite of these cookies and you will be transported into the heart of Britain. Serve these cookies with coffee or tea for the tastiest results.

**Yield:** 24 servings

**Preparation Time:** 1 hour and 35 minutes

**Ingredient List:**

- 2 cups of white flour
- ¾ cup of white sugar, extra for sprinkling
- 2 ½ teaspoons of baker's style baking powder
- 1 teaspoon of orange zest, grated
- 1 teaspoon of nutmeg, grated
- ½ teaspoons of salt
- ½ cup of butter, cold and sliced into small pieces
- ¾ cup of currants
- 2 eggs, beaten
- 2 to 3 Tablespoons of buttermilk
- Butter, melted and for greasing

HHHHHHHHHHHHHHHHHHHHHHHHHHHHHHHHHHHHHHH

**Instructions:**

1. In a medium bowl, add in the white flour, white sugar, baking powder, fresh orange zest, grated nutmeg, and dash of salt. Stir well to evenly mix.

2. Add in the butter and cut in with a pastry cutter until crumbly in consistency.

3. In a small bowl, add in the eggs and buttermilk. Whisk until lightly beaten. Add into the flour and stir well until a dough begins to form.

4. Transfer the dough into a large bowl and cover. Set aside to chill in the fridge for 1 hour.

5. Place the dough onto a flat surface that has been dusted with flour. Roll out the dough until ¼ inch in thickness. Cut 2 inch rounds out of the dough.

6. Place a griddle over low to medium heat. Grease with melted butter. Add the dough discs onto the griddle. Cook for 4 to 5 minutes on each side or until browned.

7. Remove and transfer to a wire rack to cool.

8. Sprinkle the sugar over the top of the cookies. Serve.

# About the Author

Angel Burns learned to cook when she worked in the local seafood restaurant near her home in Hyannis Port in Massachusetts as a teenager. The head chef took Angel under his wing and taught the young woman the tricks of the trade for cooking seafood. The skills she had learned at a young age helped her get accepted into Boston University's Culinary Program where she also minored in business administration.

Summers off from school meant working at the same restaurant but when Angel's mentor and friend retired as head chef, she took over after graduation and created classic and new dishes that delighted the diners. The restaurant flourished under Angel's culinary creativity and one customer developed more than an appreciation for Angel's food. Several months after taking over the position, the young woman met her future husband at work and they have been inseparable ever since. They still live in Hyannis Port with their two children and a cocker spaniel named Buddy.

Angel Burns turned her passion for cooking and her business acumen into a thriving e-book business. She has authored several successful books on cooking different types of dishes using simple ingredients for novices and experienced chefs alike. She is still head chef in Hyannis Port and says she will probably never leave!

# Author's Afterthoughts

With so many books out there to choose from, I want to thank you for choosing this one and taking precious time out of your life to buy and read my work. Readers like you are the reason I take such passion in creating these books.

It is with gratitude and humility that I express how honored I am to become a part of your life and I hope that you take the same pleasure in reading this book as I did in writing it.

Can I ask one small favour? I ask that you write an honest and open review on Amazon of what you thought of the book. This will help other readers make an informed choice on whether to buy this book.

*My sincerest thanks,*

*Angel Burns*

If you want to be the first to know about news, new books, events and giveaways, subscribe to my newsletter by clicking the link below

*https://angel-burns.gr8.com*

**or Scan QR-code**

Printed in the USA
CPSIA information can be obtained
at www.ICGtesting.com
LVHW040009070524
779557LV00034B/458